Macbeth

William Shakespeare

Illustrated by

Nick Spender

Retold by

Stephen Haynes

Series created and designed by

David Salariya

GRAFFEX

Macbeth

Artist: Nick Spender

Editorial Assistant: Mark Williams

Published in Great Britain in 2008 by
Book House, an imprint of
The Salariya Book Company Ltd
25 Marlborough Place, Brighton, BNI IUB
www.salariya.com
www.book-house.co.uk

ISBN-13: 978-1-905638-82-6 (PB)

SALARIYA

1 3 5 7 9 8 6 4 2

A CIP catalogue record for this book is available
from the British Library.

Printed and bound in China.
Printed on paper from sustainable sources.

Visit our website at **www.book-house.co.uk**
for **free** electronic versions of:
You Wouldn't Want to be an Egyptian Mummy!
You Wouldn't Want to be a Roman Gladiator!
Avoid Joining Shackleton's Polar Expedition!
Avoid Sailing on a 19th-Century Whaling Ship!

Picture credits:
p. 40 TopFoto.co.uk
p. 41 John James
p. 43 Carolyn Franklin
p. 44 © 2003 Charles Walker/TopFoto
p. 47 © 2005 TopFoto
Every effort has been made to trace copyright holders. The Salariya Book Company apologises for any omissions and would be pleased, in such cases, to add an acknowledgement in future editions.

When shall we three meet again,
in thunder, lightning, or in rain?

When the hurly-burly's done,
when the battle's lost and won.

That will be ere[1] the set of sun.

Fair is foul, and foul is fair:
hover through the fog and filthy air.

1. ere: before.

Main Characters

Macbeth,
Thane of
Glamis

Lady Macbeth

Banquo, a thane
of Scotland

Duncan,
King of Scotland

Malcolm,
Duncan's elder son

Donalbain,
Duncan's younger son

Macduff,
Thane of Fife

Lady Macduff

Lennox and Ross,
thanes of Scotland

Angus,
a thane of Scotland

The weird sisters

A NATIONAL HERO

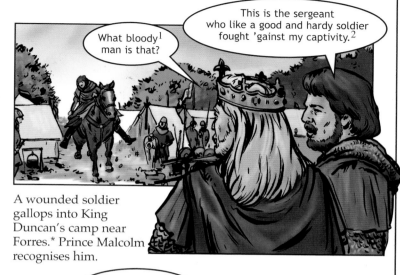

A wounded soldier gallops into King Duncan's camp near Forres.* Prince Malcolm recognises him.

The sergeant describes how Macbeth fearlessly charged through the rebels, looking for their leader.

He slew Macdonald and stuck his head on the battlements as a warning to others.

No sooner had Macbeth defeated the rebels than the King of Norway[3] attacked from the other direction.

A Scottish nobleman, the Thane[4] of Cawdor, fought on the Norwegian side, but Macbeth eventually forced them to surrender.

Duncan is furious when he hears of Cawdor's treachery.

*For place names, see the map on page 43.   1. bloody: bloodstained.   2. 'gainst my captivity: to save me from being captured.   3. Norway: Some parts of Scotland are closer to Norway than they are to England, and raids were common. 4. Thane: a rank of the Scottish nobility, slightly below an English earl.   5. present: immediate.   6. with . . . Macbeth: Tell Macbeth that he is the new Thane of Cawdor.   7. hath: has.

A PROPHECY

Where hast thou[1] been, sister?

Killing swine.

A drum, a drum! Macbeth doth come.[2]

All hail, Macbeth! Hail to thee,[4] Thane of Glamis![5]

All hail, Macbeth! Hail to thee, Thane of Cawdor!

All hail, Macbeth, that shalt[6] be king hereafter![7]

The three weird sisters[3] prepare to waylay Macbeth and Banquo as they return from their victorious campaign.

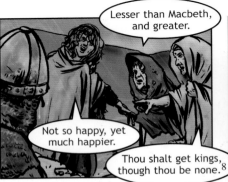

Lesser than Macbeth, and greater.

Not so happy, yet much happier.

Thou shalt get kings, though thou be none.[8]

Macbeth wants to know more.

I know I am Thane of Glamis; but how of Cawdor? And to be king stands not within the prospect of belief.[9]

Your children shall be kings.

You shall be king.

And Thane of Cawdor too: went it not so?[10]

What can this mean? Banquo asks whether the sisters have any message for him. They answer him with riddles.

But instead of answering him, the witches vanish. Macbeth and Banquo can scarcely believe what they have heard.

The king hath happily received, Macbeth, the news of thy[11] success.

He bade me,[12] from him, call thee[13] Thane of Cawdor.

What, can the devil speak true?

Glamis, and Thane of Cawdor! The greatest is behind.[14]

The Thanes of Ross and Angus come riding to meet Macbeth with a message from the king.

Angus explains that Cawdor has been sentenced to death, and his title has been given to Macbeth. Does this mean that the other prophecies might also come true?

1. hast thou: have you.   2. doth come: is coming.   3. weird sisters: witches. 'Weird' means 'to do with fate or destiny'.
4. Hail to thee: Greetings to you.   5. Glamis: usually pronounced 'glahmz'.   6. shalt: shall   7. hereafter: afterwards.
8. Thou . . . none: You will have children who are kings, but you will not be one yourself.   9. stands . . . belief: is totally
unbelievable.   10. went it not so?: isn't that what they said?   11. thy: your.   12. bade me: told me to ('bade' is usually
pronounced 'bad').   13. thee: you.   14. behind: still to come.

Why do I yield to that suggestion whose horrid image doth unfix my hair?[1]

If chance will have me king, why, chance may crown me, without my stir.[2]

Very frankly he confessed his treasons, implored your highness' pardon, and set forth a deep repentance.

Back at King Duncan's camp

Banquo warns him that the witches are messengers of the devil and cannot be trusted. But Macbeth is not listening. He *could* become king, if he dared... Or perhaps, if he is fated to be king, it will somehow just happen by itself?

Prince Malcolm reports to his father that the traitor Cawdor has been executed.

There's no art to find the mind's construction in the face.[4]

O worthiest cousin! More is thy due[5] than more than all can pay.

Nothing in his life became him[3] like the leaving it.

He was a gentleman on whom I built an absolute trust.

The heroes return, and the king congratulates them.
   But now Duncan has a most important announcement to make.

We will establish our estate upon our eldest, Malcolm, whom we name hereafter the Prince of Cumberland.[6]

That is a step on which I must fall down, or else o'erleap,[7] for in my way it lies.

Stars, hide your fires; let not light see my black and deep desires.

He has decided who should succeed him as King of Scots.

Macbeth is dismayed: this means that Malcolm, not Macbeth, is now the heir to the throne.

If he really wants to be king, he will have to seize the crown for himself.

1. unfix my hair: make my hair stand on end.   2. without my stir: without my doing anything.   3. became him: was worthy of him. In other words, his death was the most noble act of his whole life.   4. There's . . . face: There is no way to judge a person's character from their appearance.   5. More is thy due: You deserve more.   6. Prince of Cumberland: the title of the heir to the Scottish throne.   7. a step . . . o'erleap: an obstacle that will stop me unless I can get over it.

AMBITION

'My dearest partner of greatness!'

Glamis thou art,[1] and Cawdor; and shalt be what thou art promised.

Macbeth's castle at Inverness

Yet do I fear thy nature: it is too full o'th'milk of human kindness.

Macbeth has written to his wife about the witches' prophecy and his new appointment as Thane of Cawdor.

She is thrilled by the news.

But will Macbeth be ruthless enough to make sure that the prophecy comes true?

Hie thee hither,[2] that I may pour my spirits in thine ear,

and chastise with the valour of my tongue all that impedes thee from the golden round.[3]

The king comes here tonight.

Thou'rt mad to say it![4]

So please you, it is true.

It will be up to her to make sure that he is!

A servant brings the news that Duncan is on his way to Inverness.

The raven himself is hoarse that croaks the fatal entrance of Duncan under my battlements.

Come, you spirits that tend on mortal thoughts,[5] unsex me here,[6]

and fill me from the crown to the toe top-full of direst cruelty!

So her chance has come already! Duncan will be here, in her own house, at her mercy.

She must steel herself, and put any thought of pity out of her mind.

---

1. thou art: you are.   2. hie thee hither: hurry here.   3. chastise . . . round: persuade you to ignore the doubts that keep you from seizing the crown.   4. Thou'rt mad to say it!: Why is she so startled? Does she think for a moment that when the servant says 'the king' he means Macbeth? Or does she find it hard to believe that Duncan has already fallen into her hands?   5. tend on mortal thoughts: encourage thoughts of death.   6. unsex me: make me forget that I am a woman; make me as ruthless as a man.

At last Macbeth himself arrives. She greets
him by his new title for the first time.

They both have the same thought:
Duncan must die.

They must welcome Duncan graciously
and behave as though all is well. He will
suspect nothing.

1. goes hence: goes away – but it can also mean 'dies'.   2. purposes: intends.   3. put . . . into my dispatch: let me
organise it.   4. look up clear: look cheerful.   5. to alter . . . fear: changing your expression is always a sign that
you are afraid.

A ROYAL VISIT

King Duncan and his lords approach Macbeth's castle. They are charmed by the delightful, peaceful scene.

Lady Macbeth comes out to welcome them, curtseying graciously.

A magnificent feast has been prepared for the royal guest, but Macbeth has left the hall to be alone for a while. He is getting cold feet.

There are good reasons why he should not kill Duncan.

In fact, it is Macbeth's duty to protect his guest.

Lady Macbeth has come to find him. He should be entertaining his royal visitor, not skulking in the dark by himself.

Macbeth has finally made up his mind.

---

1. seat: location.   2. we are: I am. It was usual for kings and queens to call themselves 'we'; later, Macbeth will do the same.   3. If . . . done: If it could all be safely over and done with.   4. 'twere well: it would be a good thing.
5. kinsman: relative (Macbeth and Duncan are cousins).   6. I have . . . itself: The only thing that drives me on (as a spur drives a horse) is ambition, which makes me attempt too much.   7. supped: finished eating.

12

But Lady Macbeth has laid her plans and will not stop now. Where is his courage?

She would not give up so easily. She would murder her own baby, if she had to!

Now she tries to flatter him.

Her plan is to get Duncan's servants drunk, and use their daggers to kill him.

---

1. Was the hope . . . freely?: She compares him to a man who is brave when he is drunk, but not when he wakes up the next morning.   2. such . . . love: this is what I think your love for me is worth.   3. Prithee: I beg you.   4. become a man: be worthy of a man.   5. who dares . . . none: anyone who does what is unworthy of a man is not a man.   6. durst: dared. 7. screw . . . sticking-place: summon all your courage (like winding a crossbow as tight as it will go).   8. received: believed by everyone.   9. done't: done it   10. mock . . . show: trick everyone by pretending that all is well.

THE GHOSTLY DAGGER

Banquo and his son Fleance are on their way to bed
when they hear footsteps in the dark. Alarmed,
Banquo draws his sword – but it is only Macbeth.

The king has entrusted
Banquo with a
valuable gift for Lady
Macbeth

Macbeth pretends he
has forgotten about the
prophecies. They both
know this is not true.

Macbeth bids Banquo and Fleance goodnight.

Macbeth has arranged for his wife to
give a secret signal as soon as the
servants are unconscious.

14   1. withal: with.   2. when we can entreat an hour to serve: when I have time to spare. Macbeth is already using the 'royal plural' – saying 'we' when he means 'I'.   3. the while: meanwhile.   4. the like: the same.

Is this a dagger which I see before me, the handle toward my hand?

Left alone in the darkened castle, Macbeth is suddenly confronted with a ghostly apparition.

I have thee not, and yet I see thee still.

Art thou but a dagger of the mind?

He tries to take hold of it but his hand goes straight through.

I see thee still, and on thy blade and dudgeon[1] gouts[2] of blood, which was not so before.

It seems to be leading him towards Duncan's bedchamber. As he follows it, he sees drops of blood glistening on it.

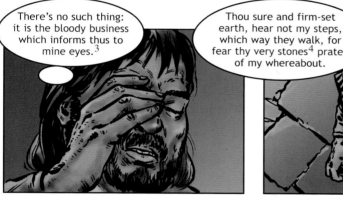

There's no such thing: it is the bloody business which informs thus to mine eyes.[3]

Thou sure and firm-set earth, hear not my steps, which way they walk, for fear thy very stones[4] prate[5] of my whereabout.

He rubs his eyes, and the dagger vanishes.

He treads as quietly as he can, afraid that any sound on the flagstones may give him away.

TING!

I go, and it is done;[6] the bell invites me.

Behind him, the bell rings quietly, as planned.

Hear it not, Duncan; for it is a knell[7] that summons thee to heaven or to hell.

1. dudgeon: handle.   2. gouts: drops   3. it is . . . eyes: the thought of murder is making me see things that are not real.   4. thy very stones: even your stones.   5. prate: tell tales.   6. I go . . . done: As soon as I go, it will be over and done with.   7. knell: funeral bell.

THE DEED IS DONE

Lady Macbeth is waiting for her husband to come back after killing Duncan. The suspense is unbearable; the slightest noise alarms her. A voice calls out in a distant corridor. Who can it be?

She has drugged the servants and put their daggers where Macbeth could find them – what could go wrong?

Only one thing stopped her from killing Duncan herself.

The door creaks open.

Both of them are on edge.

Macbeth has blood on his hands.

Somewhere in the castle, he heard someone wake.

Lady Macbeth has no time for this nonsense.

---

1. He is about it: He is doing it now.   2. alack: alas.   3. 'tis: it is.   4. I had done't: I would have done it.   5. Ay: yes.
6. methought: it seemed to me.   7. knits . . . care: cures us of our everyday worries, as if it was mending a frayed garment.   8. witness: evidence.

She suddenly notices that Macbeth is still carrying the servants' daggers. He was supposed to leave them as incriminating evidence!

As Lady Macbeth goes to return the daggers, there is a loud knocking at the castle gate.

Lady Macbeth has returned from planting the daggers.

1. Infirm of purpose: indecisive, easily discouraged.   2. but as pictures: only like pictures.   3. 'tis . . . devil: only children are afraid of a picture of something frightening.   4. whence: from where.   5. How is't with me?: What's the matter with me?   6. appals: frightens.   7. Neptune: Roman god of the sea.   8. multitudinous: many, vast.   9. incarnadine: stain red.   10. I would thou couldst: I wish you could.

O Horror, Horror, Horror!

The gatekeeper finally arrives to see who is knocking.
He has enjoyed the feast, and had far too much to drink.

Macduff and Lennox have arrived early to call on the
king. As they step through the gate, Macbeth comes
to meet them, pulling his cloak around him to make
them think he has just woken up.

While Macduff goes to see the king,
Lennox tells Macbeth that he and
Macduff have not slept well. But then
a sudden shout rings through the castle.

Macduff comes rushing back
from the king's chamber with
the most dreadful news.

Macbeth and Lennox rush off to see for themselves,
while Macduff rouses the whole household. Lady
Macbeth and Banquo are the first to arrive.

---

1. porter: gatekeeper   2. old: a lot of.   3. anon: soon (in other words, 'I'm coming!').   4. stirring: awake.
5. timely: early.   6. i'th': in the.   7. 'twas: it was.   8. sacrilegious: hateful to God. (In Shakespeare's time it was
believed that kings were chosen by God.)   9. bid me: ask me to.   10. alarum: alarm.

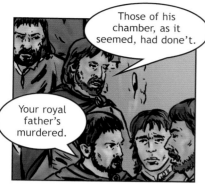

Those of his chamber, as it seemed, had done't.

Your royal father's murdered.

O, yet I do repent me of my fury, that I did kill them.

Wherefore[1] did you so?

Who can be wise, amazed, temp'rate[2] and furious, loyal and neutral, in a moment? No man.[3]

Help me hence, ho!

Look to the lady.

Macduff breaks the news to Duncan's sons, Malcolm and Donalbain. Lennox, having examined the crime scene, is convinced by Macbeth's alibi.

While Macbeth struggles to answer Macduff's awkward question, Lady Macbeth creates a diversion by pretending to feel faint.

Where we are, there's daggers in men's smiles.

And Duncan's horses — a thing most strange and certain — turned wild in nature.

'Tis said they eat[4] each other.

They did so.

Is't known who did this more than bloody[5] deed?

Those that Macbeth hath slain.

Duncan's sons are afraid that they will be killed next. They decide to flee.

Later that day, as Macduff is leaving the castle, he finds Ross and an old man discussing the strange omens that have been reported.

Then 'tis most like[6] the sovereignty[7] will fall upon Macbeth.

Will you to[10] Scone?

The king's two sons are stol'n away and fled, which puts upon them suspicion of the deed.

He is already named, and gone to Scone[8] to be invested.[9]

No, cousin, I'll to Fife.

God's benison[11] go with you.

But now the sudden departure of Malcolm and Donalbain has given Macbeth a further alibi.

Macduff has decided not to attend Macbeth's coronation. He is going home instead.

1. wherefore: why. 2. temp'rate: temperate, calm. 3. Who . . . no man: When you are astonished and angry, you cannot behave wisely and calmly; if you are loyal to your king, you cannot forget your loyalty. Macbeth is pretending that he was so angry with the servants that he could not help killing them. 4.eat: ate. 5. bloody: bloodthirsty. 6. like: likely. 7. sovereignty: kingship. 8. Scone: the ancient capital of Scotland, where the King of Scots was traditionally crowned. 9. invested: made king in a special ceremony. 10. Will you to: Will you go to. 11. benison: blessing.

A CONTRACT TO KILL

...and I fear thou play'dst most foully for't.[1]

Thou hast it now: King, Cawdor, Glamis, all, as the weird women promised...

Macbeth and his lady have been crowned at Scone. The witches' prophecy to Macbeth has been fulfilled. Banquo is beginning to be suspicious.

Yet it was said... myself should be the root and father of many kings.

Here's our chief guest.

Tonight we hold a solemn supper, sir, and I'll request your presence.

But what of their prediction for Banquo – that his descendants will inherit the throne?

Macbeth is planning a grand feast to celebrate his coronation, and Banquo is to be the guest of honour.

Ride you this afternoon?

Ay, my good lord.

Fail not[2] our feast.

My lord, I will not.

We hear our bloody cousins are bestowed[3] in England and in Ireland, not confessing their cruel parricide,[4] filling their hearers with strange invention.[5]

But first Banquo has a journey to make.

The official story now is that Malcolm and Donalbain are the killers.

---

1. play'dst . . . for't: got it by unfair means.   2. fail not: do not miss.   3. bestowed: hidden away.
4. parricide: the murder of their own father.   5. strange invention: made-up stories. (No doubt they are telling people that Macbeth is the murderer.)

Banquo and his young son mount their horses.

Macbeth realises that Banquo has behaved more wisely than he has.

And he has not forgotten the prediction about Banquo's children.

He has arranged a secret meeting with two desperate characters.

He wants Banquo killed, but it must be done secretly. Fleance must die too.

1. To be . . . safely thus: It is no use being king unless you are safely king.   2. rubs nor botches: mistakes.
3. thy soul's . . . tonight: If heaven is where your soul is going, it will go there tonight.

A Botched Job

King Macbeth and his queen are not enjoying their new status at all. They live in constant fear, and are tormented by nightmares.

Duncan is better off than they are – he no longer has anything to worry about.

But Macbeth's plan is underway...

---

1. Nought's had . . . content: When we get what we wanted and are still not happy, we have gained nothing for our trouble.   2. Things . . . regard: There is no point worrying about things that cannot be changed.   3. let . . . disjoint: let the whole world fall apart.   4. both the worlds: heaven and earth.   5. ere: before, rather than.   6. Be innocent . . . deed: You had better not know about it yet, but you will be pleased once it is done.

Light thickens,
and the crow makes wing[1] to th'rooky wood;
good things of day begin to droop and drowse,
while night's black agents to their preys do rouse.[2]

Outside the castle, as night falls

Hark! I hear horses.

The two murderers lie in wait for Banquo and Fleance as they return to the castle. Macbeth has sent a third man to give them their instructions – and perhaps to keep an eye on them as well.

It will be rain tonight.

Let it come down!

Banquo and Fleance, suspecting nothing, dismount from their horses to walk to the castle gate.

O, treachery!
Fly, good Fleance, fly, fly, fly!
Thou mayst revenge.

Who did strike out the light?

Was't not the way?[3]

There's but one down;[4] the son is fled.

1. makes wing: flies. 2. rouse: awake. 3. Was't . . . way?: Wasn't that the plan? 4. but one down: only one killed.

BANQUO RETURNS

The new king and queen have put on a splendid banquet for the Scottish noblemen. But Macbeth is not at the table; he has spotted one of the murderers lurking in the shadows by the door.

But the murder has not gone according to plan.

Fleance will be dangerous one day – and his descendants could be kings!

Lady Macbeth has called him back to the feast.

But when Macbeth goes to sit down, he finds his seat taken! Banquo has come to the feast after all – just as he promised.

1. dispatched: got rid of.   2. venom: poison. Once he is grown up, Fleance will be as dangerous to Macbeth as a poisonous snake, because he will want revenge.   3. gory locks: bloodstained hair.

The guests do not know what to think;
they cannot see what Macbeth is staring at.

Now that the ghost has
gone, Macbeth pulls
himself together and
proposes a toast.

But as soon as Banquo's
name is mentioned, the ghost
reappears. Lady Macbeth has
to send the guests away.

1. thus: like this.   2. upon a thought: in no time at all.   3. painting of your fear: hallucination caused by fear.
4. you look but on: you are only looking at.   5. would: I wish.   6. Avaunt: Go away.   7. Stand . . . going: Don't insist
on leaving in the proper order (with the most important people going first).

STIRRINGS OF REBELLION

It will have blood; they say blood will have blood.

The embarrassed guests have gone, leaving Macbeth and his Lady alone.

How sayst thou, that Macduff denies his person[1] at our great bidding?

Did you send to him,[2] sir?

I hear it by the way, but I will send.

Macduff was invited to the feast; why didn't he come?

There's not a one of them but in his house I keep a servant fee'd.[3]

Macbeth has spies everywhere; he no longer trusts anyone.

I will tomorrow — and betimes[4] I will — to the weird sisters. More shall they speak.

He wants no more uncertainty. He has resolved to find out the worst – by confronting the three sisters once more.

I am in blood stepped in so far that, should I wade no more, returning were[5] as tedious as go o'er.

We are yet but young in deed.[6]

Now that he has so many deaths on his conscience, there is no turning back.

Meanwhile, in a secret place...

How did you dare to trade and traffic[7] with Macbeth in riddles and affairs of death?

Hecate, goddess of sorcery, is angry with the weird sisters. They should have consulted her before meddling with Macbeth's destiny.

He shall spurn[8] fate, scorn death, and bear his hopes 'bove wisdom, grace and fear.

And you all know, security[9] is mortals' chiefest enemy.

They must encourage Macbeth in his evil plans. In the end, he will go too far – and bring about his own destruction.

1. How . . . person: What do you think of the fact that Macduff refuses to come?   2. send to him: send a messenger to him (to find out why).   3. fee'd: paid.   4. betimes: early.   5. were: would be. Like a man wading through a river, he has gone so far that going back would be just as difficult as going on.   6. We are . . . deed: We still have much more to do/We are not yet used to doing these things.   7. traffic: deal.   8. spurn: scorn.   9. security: thinking you are safe.

Things have been strangely borne.[1] The gracious Duncan was pitied of Macbeth — marry,[2] he was dead.

And the right-valiant Banquo walked too late; whom you may say, if't please you, Fleance killed, for Fleance fled.

Men must not walk too late.

Meanwhile, far from Macbeth's castle...

Lennox and another lord are discussing the sorry state that Scotland is in now that Macbeth has become king. Everyone knows who is responsible for the mysterious deaths, but no-one dares to say so.

Some people pretend to think that Fleance killed Banquo and ran away.

How it did grieve Macbeth! Did he not straight[4] in pious[5] rage the two delinquents tear?

Was not that nobly done?

And 'cause he failed his presence at the tyrant's feast, I hear Macduff lives in disgrace.

Who cannot want the thought[3] how monstrous it was for Malcolm and for Donalbain to kill their gracious father?

Others say that Malcolm and Donalbain killed their own father. Or is it the two murdered servants who are supposed to be guilty?

And now Macduff is suspected because he refused to attend the feast.

I'll send my prayers with him.

The other lord has news of Macduff: he is in England, trying to persuade King Edward the Confessor and the Earl of Northumberland to fight against Macbeth.

1. borne: done, carried out.   2. marry: a mild oath.   3. Who . . . thought: Everyone is bound to think.
4. straight: straight away.   5. pious: virtuous.

A Vision of the Future

Hecate looks on as the weird sisters brew their gruesome potion.

Thrice the brindled[1] cat hath mewed.

Thrice and once the hedge-pig[2] whined.

Harpier[3] cries, ''Tis time, 'tis time!'

Double, double toil and trouble; fire burn and cauldron bubble!

Fillet of a fenny[4] snake, in the cauldron boil and bake; eye of newt and toe of frog, wool of bat and tongue of dog.

Double, double toil and trouble; fire burn and cauldron bubble!

By the pricking of my thumbs, something wicked this way comes.[5]

How now, you secret, black, and midnight hags! What is't you do?

A deed without a name.

Macbeth has come to find out more about the future.

I conjure you,[6] by that which you profess,[7] howe'er you come to know it, answer me.

Say if thou'dst rather hear it from our mouths, or from our masters'.

Macbeth, Macbeth, Macbeth! Beware Macduff; beware the Thane of Fife.[8]

Macbeth, Macbeth, Macbeth! Be bloody,[9] bold, and resolute.[10]

Call 'em; let me see 'em.

Whate'er thou art, for thy good caution, thanks.

Laugh to scorn[11] the power of man, for none of woman born[12] shall harm Macbeth.

He demands to know the whole truth, come what may. He is not afraid to face any evil spirits.

Throwing more grisly ingredients into their cauldron, the witches conjure up a fearsome apparition.

As the first apparition vanishes, a second arises from the fuming cauldron.

1. brindled: with dark stripes.   2. hedge-pig: hedgehog.   3. Harpier: the name of an evil spirit.   4. fenny: from a marshy place.   5. By . . . comes: Macbeth is now so evil that even the witches feel their skin tingle when he is near.
6. conjure you: solemnly call upon you.   7. profess: believe in.   8. Thane of Fife: Macduff.   9. bloody: bloodthirsty.
10. resolute: firm.   11. laugh to scorn: think nothing of.   12. none of woman born: this usually means 'no mortal man'.

Then live, Macduff — what need I fear of thee?

But yet I'll make assurance double sure: thou shalt not live.

That will never be!

Macbeth shall never vanquished be until Great Birnam Wood to high Dunsinane hill shall come against him.

Shall Banquo's issue[1] ever reign in this kingdom?

So Macbeth need fear no mortal man! But he will take no chances: Macduff must die.

A third apparition emerges.

But there is one more thing he must know.

In answer to his question, the witches conjure up a royal procession.[2]

Thou art too like the spirit of Banquo. Down! Thy crown does sear mine eyeballs.

Filthy hags, why do you show me this?

What, will the line stretch out to th'crack of doom?[3]

And yet the eighth appears, who bears a glass which shows me many more.

Now I see 'tis true, for the blood-boltered[4] Banquo smiles upon me, and points at them for his.

What, is this so?

Ay, sir, all this is so.

1. issue: children, descendants. 2. royal procession: see page 42.
3. crack of doom: end of the world. 4. blood-boltered: bloodstained.

A MASSACRE OF INNOCENTS

The witches and their apparitions vanish, and Macbeth is puzzled to find himself suddenly alone with the Thane of Lennox.

So Macbeth's suspicions are confirmed, and this time he will not hesitate: he will wipe out the entire family.

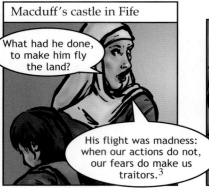

Ross has come to warn Lady Macduff that her husband has fled to England. She is shocked.

Did he go because he was afraid, or was it part of a plan?

Lady Macduff is outraged at the thought that her husband has deserted them.

But Ross believes that Macduff had good reasons for going to England.

---

1. Came they not by you?: Didn't they pass you? 2. trace him in his line: are descended from him.
3. when . . . traitors: even when we have done nothing wrong, people think we are traitors because we run away in fear.
4. wants: lacks.   5. diminutive: tiny.   6. her young ones in her nest: when she has her young ones in her nest.
7. judicious: able to make wise decisions.   8. the fits o'th'season: the way things are now.

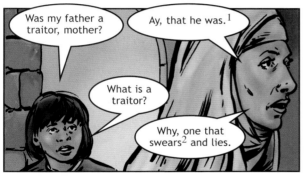

The little boy is puzzled by all this talk of traitors.

They are interrupted by a messenger who rushes in unannounced.

There is no time to run:
already Macbeth's
henchmen are at the door.

1. that he was: in law, Macduff is a traitor because he is conspiring against his king; but Lady Macduff probably means that he has betrayed his family by leaving them behind.   2. swears: makes a promise on oath.   3. hence: away from here.   4. whither: where to.   5. fry: offspring.

THE NEXT KING OF SCOTLAND?

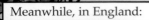

Meanwhile, in England:

This tyrant,[1] whose sole name blisters our tongues,[2] was once thought honest.

You have loved him well — he hath not touched you yet.[3]

Why in that rawness[4] left you wife and child, those strong knots of love, without leave-taking?

Malcolm and Macduff are at the court of King Edward the Confessor – a man so saintly, they say, that he can heal the sick by touching them.

Malcolm is suspicious of Macduff because he fled Scotland so suddenly, leaving his wife and children behind.

Bleed, bleed, poor country! I would not be the villain that thou think'st.

When I shall tread upon the tyrant's head, or wear it on my sword, yet my poor country shall have more vices than it had before.

Not in the legions of horrid hell can come a devil more damned in evils to top Macbeth.

Macduff has no answer to this; he can only reply that he is loyal to Scotland.

Malcolm believes that both Scotland and England will support his claim to be king. But he has a terrible confession to make: he thinks he would be an even worse king than Macbeth. Macduff cannot believe this.

I grant him bloody[5]...

We have willing dames enough.

So Malcolm decides to confess everything to him.

Malcolm cannot stop chasing after women. Macduff says this is a shame – but many women would be happy to be loved by a king.

And he cannot control his greed. Macduff says this is worse; but Scotland is a rich country, and can cope with a greedy king.

1. tyrant: cruel ruler.   2. whose . . . tongues: whose name we hate to speak.
3. he hath not touched you yet: Neither of them know yet what has happened to Macduff's family.
4. in that rawness: without protection.   5. I grant him bloody: I agree that he is bloodthirsty.

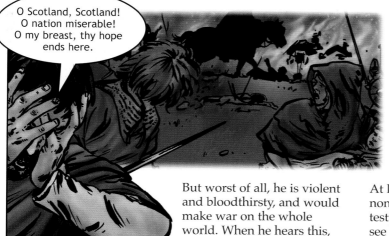

O Scotland, Scotland! O nation miserable! O my breast, thy hope ends here.

What I am truly is thine, and my poor country's, to command.

But worst of all, he is violent and bloodthirsty, and would make war on the whole world. When he hears this, Macduff is in despair.

At last Malcolm admits that none of this is true: he has been testing Macduff, and now he can see that Macduff has the good of Scotland at heart.

Stands Scotland where it did?[1]

How does my wife?

Alas, poor country!

Why, well.

And all my children?

Well, too.

They were well at peace when I did leave 'em.

Your castle is surprised; your wife and babes savagely slaughtered.

Gracious England hath lent us good Siward and ten thousand men.

Merciful heaven!

The Thane of Ross arrives with news from Scotland. But he cannot bear to tell Macduff the truth.

Malcolm tells Ross that the English have offered to help him defeat Macbeth.

At last Ross summons up the courage to tell Macduff what has happened.

All my pretty ones? Did you say all? What, all my pretty chickens and their dam[2] at one fell swoop?

Did heaven look on, and would not take their part?[3]

Within my sword's length set him; if he 'scape, heaven forgive him too.

He swears to fight for Malcolm and to kill Macbeth himself.

1. Stands . . . did?: Is Scotland still in the same state?   2. dam: mother.   3. take their part: be on their side.

CONSCIENCE

Macbeth's castle at Dunsinane

You see her eyes are open.

Ay, but their sense are shut.

For some time now, Lady Macbeth has been sleepwalking. One of her ladies in waiting is so alarmed that she has asked the doctor to come and see for himself.

Yet here's a spot. Out, damned spot! Out, I say!

Lady Macbeth goes through the motions of washing her hands. She has been doing this every night.

Fie, my lord, fie! A soldier, and afeard?[1]

Hell is murky.

What need we fear who knows it, when none can call our power to account?[2]

Again she scolds Macbeth for his lack of courage.

The Thane of Fife[3] had a wife. Where is she now? What, will these hands ne'er be clean?

Yet who would have thought the old man to have had so much blood in him?

She is reliving all their past crimes.

You have known what you should not.

She has spoke what she should not, I am sure of that. Heaven knows what she has known.

1. afeard: afraid.   2. none . . . account: there is no-one who can hold us responsible for what we have done.
3. Thane of Fife: Macduff.

This disease is beyond my practice.[1]

Wash your hands, put on your nightgown; look not so pale.

Here's the smell of the blood still; all the perfumes of Arabia will not sweeten this little hand.

O, O, O!

I tell you yet again, Banquo's buried; he cannot come out on's[2] grave.

More needs she the divine than the physician.[3] God, God forgive us all!

To bed, to bed! There's knocking at the gate. What's done cannot be undone. To bed, to bed, to bed!

She is beyond the doctor's help.

The English power[4] is near, led on by Malcolm, his uncle Siward, and the good Macduff.

Near Birnam wood shall we well meet[5] them; that way are they coming.

Now does he feel his secret murders sticking on his hands.

Near Birnam Wood

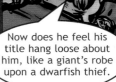

The thanes of Scotland are now in open rebellion against the tyrant Macbeth. They are on their way to Birnam Wood to meet the English army which has been sent to help them.

Now does he feel his title hang loose about him, like a giant's robe upon a dwarfish thief.

1. practice: professional skill or experience.   2. on's: of his.   3. More . . . physician: She needs a priest more than she needs a doctor.   4. power: army   5. well meet: welcome.

MACBETH STANDS ALONE

News has reached Macbeth that the Scottish thanes are moving against him.

He remembers the witches' last two prophecies.

A servant comes in with even more bad news. He is so afraid of Macbeth that he can hardly speak.

Seyton, Macbeth's adjutant, arrives. The doctor has also been summoned.

---

1. let them fly all: I don't care if everyone deserts me.   2. taint with: be weakened by.   3. sere: withered.
4. look: expect.   5. Seyton: Some experts believe that this name was pronounced like 'Satan' in Shakespeare's time.
6. Not . . . fancies: She is not physically ill, but disturbed by wild imaginings which come one after the other.
7. minister: give medical treatment.   8. therein: in this kind of illness.   9. physic: medicine.   10. I'll none of it: I'll
have nothing to do with it.   11. bane: destruction.

At Birnam Wood

Let every soldier hew him down a bough,[1] and bear't before him.

Malcolm, Macduff and Siward's English army arrive at Birnam Wood. Malcolm orders the soldiers to camouflage themselves with branches.

Back at Dunsinane

She should have died hereafter; there would have been a time for such a word.

The queen, my lord, is dead.

Tomorrow, and tomorrow, and tomorrow creeps in this petty pace[2] from day to day, to the last syllable of recorded time;

and all our yesterdays have lighted fools the way to dusty death.

Out, out, brief candle!

Life's but a walking shadow, a poor player[3] that struts and frets[4] his hour upon the stage and then is heard no more.

Macbeth is getting the castle ready to withstand a siege, when he suddenly hears the wailing of women.

It is a tale told by an idiot, full of sound and fury, signifying nothing.

As I did stand my watch upon the hill, I looked toward Birnam, and anon,[5] methought, the wood began to move.

Liar and slave!

A messenger arrives with news that is so bizarre, he hardly knows where to start.

Ring the alarum-bell! Blow wind, come wrack;[6] at least we'll die with harness[7] on our back.

1. hew . . . bough: cut down a branch for himself.   2. in this petty pace: slowly, step by step. He is saying that the future will trickle away as uselessly as the past.   3. player: actor.   4. frets: worries, fusses.   5. anon: presently, after a while.   6. wrack: destruction.   7. harness: armour.

DEATH OF A TYRANT

The army approaches Dunsinane.

Now near enough; your leafy screens throw down.

Make all our trumpets speak; give them all breath, those clamorous harbingers[1] of blood and death.

What is thy name?

Thou'lt be afraid to hear it.

Young Siward, the Earl of Northumberland's son, is the first to confront Macbeth.

My name's Macbeth.

The devil himself could not pronounce a title more hateful to mine ear.

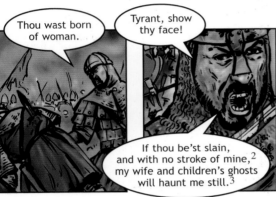

Thou wast born of woman.

Tyrant, show thy face!

If thou be'st slain, and with no stroke of mine,[2] my wife and children's ghosts will haunt me still.[3]

Macbeth easily kills the inexperienced young warrior.

Macduff is determined to kill Macbeth himself. He will not fight anyone else.

Of all men else I have avoided thee.

Turn, hell-hound, turn!

At last he finds the man he has been seeking.

But get thee back — my soul is too much charged[4] with blood of thine already.

I have no words. My voice is in my sword, thou bloodier villain than terms can give thee out.[5]

Thou losest labour.[6] I bear a charmèd[7] life, which must not yield[8] to one of woman born.

---

1. clamorous harbingers: noisy messengers.   2. If . . . mine: If you are killed by anyone other than me.   3. still: always, for ever.   4. charged: burdened   5. bloodier . . . than terms can give thee out: more bloodthirsty than words can say.   6. Thou losest labour: You're wasting your time.   7. charmèd: protected by magic.   8. yield: give way.

I'll not fight with thee.

I will try the last.

Despair thy charm — Macduff was from his mother's womb untimely[1] ripped.

Then yield thee, coward, and live to be the show and gaze o'th'time.[2]

We'll have thee, as our rarer monsters are, painted on a pole, and underwrit,[3] 'Here may you see the tyrant.'

Lay on, Macduff, and damned be him that first cries, 'Hold, enough!'[4]

The courtyard of the castle

Had he his hurts before?[5]

Ay, on the front.

Had I as many sons as I have hairs, I would not wish them to a fairer death.

The battle is over, and the castle has surrendered without a fight. Only now does Siward learn that his son is dead.

Hail, king — for so thou art.

Behold where stands th'usurper's[6] cursèd head. The time is free.[7]

Macduff presents Malcolm with a grisly trophy.

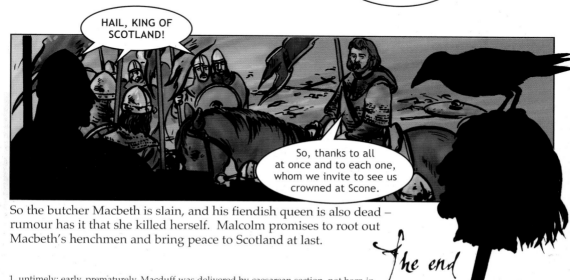

HAIL, KING OF SCOTLAND!

So, thanks to all at once and to each one, whom we invite to see us crowned at Scone.

So the butcher Macbeth is slain, and his fiendish queen is also dead — rumour has it that she killed herself. Malcolm promises to root out Macbeth's henchmen and bring peace to Scotland at last.

The end

1. untimely: early, prematurely. Macduff was delivered by caesarean section, not born in the ordinary way. 2. the show . . . time: a sideshow for people to come and look at. 3. underwrit: with a notice underneath. 4. 'Hold, enough!': 'I give up!' 5. Had . . . before?: Was he wounded on the front (like a brave man)? 6. usurper: one who wrongly seizes the crown. 7. The time is free: This is a time of freedom.

William Shakespeare was born in Stratford-upon-Avon, Warwickshire, England, in 1564, possibly on 23 April, which is St George's Day – the feast-day of England's patron saint. His father was a respected businessman who became mayor of Stratford, though it seems he never learned to write. We know nothing of William's childhood and education, except that he did not go to university. He probably learned Latin at the King's New School in Stratford.

In 1582 he married Anne Hathaway. He was only 18; she was 26, and pregnant. Their daughter Susanna was born 6 months later, and in 1585 they had twins, Hamnet and Judith. Anne and the children seem to have stayed in Stratford all their lives, even while William was living and working in London.

LONDON AND THE THEATRE

Shakespeare was acting and writing plays in London by about 1590. We do not know how he made his living before that, or how he got started as a playwright. London in the 1590s was an exciting place for anyone interested in the stage. Theatres – or 'playhouses' – were not allowed in the City of London itself; they were built on the north side of London, outside the city walls, and in Southwark, on the south bank of the Thames. Many playwrights were active in London at this time. Christopher Marlowe wrote several blockbuster tragedies before being killed in a brawl at the age of 29. Other well-known writers included Thomas Dekker,

MR. WILLIAM
SHAKESPEARES
COMEDIES,
HISTORIES, &
TRAGEDIES.
Published according to the True Originall Copies.

LONDON
Printed by Isaac Iaggard, and Ed. Blount. 1623.

Portrait of Shakespeare by Martin Droeshout, on the title-page of the First Folio edition of Shakespeare's plays (London, 1623)

Thomas Kyd, John Webster, Thomas Middleton, and the partnership of Francis Beaumont and John Fletcher. In the 1600s, Ben Jonson wrote a series of clever and witty comedies; Shakespeare acted in some of them.

Writing plays was not an especially well-paid job – the author's fee might be less than the value of an actor's costume. But Shakespeare was a keen businessman. In 1594 he became a shareholder in a new acting company, the Lord Chamberlain's Men. This meant that he invested money in the company, and in return he was paid a share of the profits made by the

company. With the money he made, he was able to buy land in Stratford for his family, and a magnificent house, New Place. He also became a shareholder in the new Globe theatre, which opened in 1599.

SHAKESPEARE AND JAMES I

In 1603 Queen Elizabeth I died and James VI of Scotland became James I of England. James was keen on the theatre, and he changed the name of the Lord Chamberlain's Men to the King's Men. Some time after this – perhaps in 1606 – Shakespeare wrote *Macbeth*, his only play on a Scottish subject. The play must have been especially interesting to the new king. James was an expert on witchcraft, and believed in the 'divine right of kings' – in other words, he thought that kings were chosen by God and that killing a king was a particularly evil crime. James also

believed that his family, the Stuarts, were descended from Banquo, Thane of Lochaber, a Scottish nobleman killed by Macbeth in the 11th century.

SHAKESPEARE'S WORKS

Shakespeare wrote about 39 plays (experts disagree about the exact number), four long poems and 154 sonnets (short poems of 14 lines). After 1614 he seems to have retired from the theatre and spent most of his time in Stratford. He died there on St George's Day, 1616.

Only about half his plays were published in his lifetime, but in 1623 two of his theatrical friends published a deluxe edition of 36 plays. This very valuable book is known today as the First Folio. Since then he has come to be regarded as the greatest playwright in the English language – perhaps in any language.

A cutaway view of the Globe theatre in Southwark, London, where many of Shakespeare's plays were first performed.

A copy of the Globe was completed in 1997, close to the original site, and Shakespeare's plays (amongst others) are regularly performed there.

THE REAL MACBETH

There really was a King Macbeth in 11th-century Scotland, but his true story is very different from Shakespeare's version of it. Shakespeare's Macbeth is Thane of Glamis, but the real Macbeth was Mormaer of Moray – a very much more important title. He ruled a large area of northern Scotland, much bigger than present-day Moray.

The King of Scots from 1034 was Duncan I, a young and unsuccessful ruler. In 1040, after trying to attack the English city of Durham, Duncan invaded Macbeth's territory of Moray. He was defeated by Macbeth at the battle of Pitgaveny near Elgin, and died from his wounds. Macbeth was then proclaimed King of Scots, while Duncan's sons went into exile. In Scotland at this time it was usual for the new king to be chosen from the cousins or nephews of the old king. Macbeth was a member of the royal family and had a good claim to the throne.

Macbeth ruled Scotland for 17 years, from 1040 to 1057, and his reign was mainly peaceful. He and his wife, Gruoch, donated money to the Church, and in 1050 Macbeth even went on pilgrimage to Rome, where he gave generously to the poor.

In 1054 an English army under Earl Siward of Northumbria invaded Scotland and Macbeth's power was broken. He was finally defeated at the battle of Lumphanan in 1057 by Duncan's son, Malcolm Canmore, and died of his wounds a few days later. His stepson Lulach became king, but lasted less than a year. Malcolm Canmore (his surname means 'Great Chief') then ruled Scotland as Malcolm III from 1058 to 1093.

THE STUART DYNASTY

In the play, Macbeth has his friend Banquo murdered, but Banquo's son Fleance escapes. King James believed he was descended from Fleance, who went into exile in England. When Macbeth visits the witches for the last time, they conjure up a procession of the eight Stuart kings of Scotland (Mary, Queen of Scots is left out):

Robert II	reigned 1371–1390
Robert III	1390–1406
James I	1406–1437
James II	1437–1460
James III	1460–1488
James IV	1488–1513
James V	1513–1542
James VI	1567–1625

James VI carries a 'glass' which shows all the other Stuart kings into the distant future. At the time, everyone expected that the next king would be James's son Henry. He was a handsome and popular young man, and there was great sadness when he died suddenly of typhoid fever at the age of 18. In fact, there were five Stuart rulers after James:

Charles I	1625–1649
Charles II	1660–1685*
James II	1685–1688
Mary II	1689–1694**
Anne	1702–1714

There was no king during the Civil War and Commonwealth period, 1649–1660.
**Joint ruler with William III (1689–1702).*

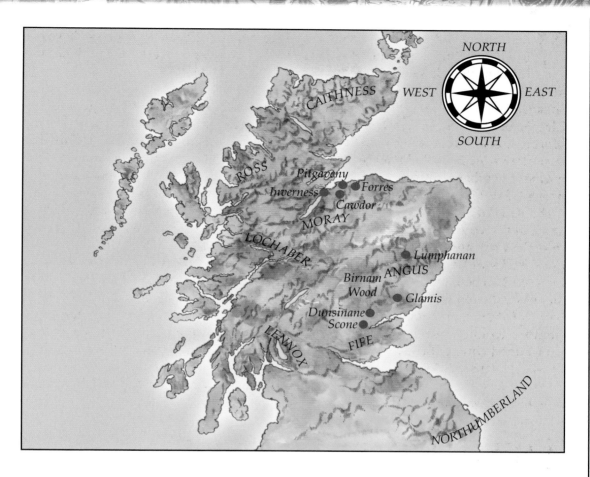

SCOTLAND AND ENGLAND

*U*ntil the 18th century, England and Scotland were two separate kingdoms – and they were not always friendly. In 1587 Queen Elizabeth I of England executed the ex-Queen of Scots, Mary Stuart. Elizabeth was a Protestant, Mary a Roman Catholic, and Elizabeth was convinced that Mary was plotting against her.

But Elizabeth had no children, so when she died in 1603 there was no English prince or princess to take her place. Instead, the English crown was offered to Elizabeth's cousin, King James VI of Scotland – the son of her old enemy, Mary, Queen of Scots. He is often referred to as 'James the First and Sixth', because he was James I of England and James VI of Scotland.

James wanted to join England and Scotland together to make one country called Great Britain, but the English and Scottish parliaments would not allow this. So – even though they shared the same king – Scotland and England remained separate kingdoms for another hundred years. They were finally united in 1707, and Queen Anne – the last ruler of the Stuart dynasty – became the first Queen of Great Britain.

In Shakespeare's time, even educated people could believe in witchcraft. James I and VI wrote a book on the subject, *Demonology*, in 1597. Here are some of the things that Shakespeare's contemporaries believed about witches:

- They could be male or female, but most of them were women.
- They had meetings with the devil.
- They kept pets which were really evil spirits in disguise.
- They could foretell the future; in particular, they knew when a person was going to die.
- They could kill people and animals from a distance.
- They could hurt people by sticking pins into a dummy.
- They could fly.
- They could sail the sea in a sieve.
- They could control the weather.

Even people who tried to do good might be accused of witchcraft – including those who treated the sick with herbal medicines and Christian prayers. Midwives – nurses who help women in childbirth – were often accused.

THE NORTH BERWICK WITCHES

In 1589 James married Princess Anne, the sister of King Christian IV of Denmark. The plan was that Anne would sail from Denmark to Scotland for the wedding – but her ship was battered by storms and forced to land in Norway. Eventually James sailed to Norway himself and married her there. But the voyage home was rough and the ship nearly sank.

King James attending the North Berwick witch trials; a hand-coloured woodcut from the 1591 edition of the pamphlet News from Scotland

James was convinced that these storms were caused by witches. There was a witch-hunt in Denmark, and two Danish women were burnt at the stake. Then a number of people were accused in Scotland, at North Berwick near Edinburgh. James himself helped to interrogate some of them. They were tortured, and confessed to amazing crimes such as kissing the devil's backside. They were sentenced to death by burning or strangling. Some historians think that as many as 4,000 people were executed for witchcraft in Scotland between 1560 and 1707 – and many more in England, America and other 'civilised' countries.

We don't know whether Shakespeare believed in witches or not. But the witches in *Macbeth* were certainly the most popular part of the play. After Shakespeare's death, Thomas Middleton wrote extra scenes for the witches, with singing and dancing. Modern editions of the play still include some lines which are probably by Middleton rather than Shakespeare.

1564
William Shakespeare born in Stratford-upon-Avon, Warwickshire. Elizabeth I has been Queen of England since 1558. Mary Stuart has been Queen of Scots since 1542.

1565
Mary, Queen of Scots marries her second husband, Lord Darnley.

1566
Mary's secretary David Rizzio is murdered. Mary gives birth to the future King James VI of Scotland, who will also become James I of England.

1567
Lord Darnley is murdered. Mary is abducted by the Earl of Bothwell and marries him. She is imprisoned and forced to abdicate the Scottish throne; James VI becomes King of Scots, aged 1.

1568
Mary escapes to England where she is again imprisoned, accused of the murder of Darnley.

1577
First edition of Raphael Holinshed's *Chronicles of England, Scotland and Ireland*, Shakespeare's main source for the story of Macbeth. Francis Drake sets out to sail round the world on the *Golden Hind* (returns 1580).

1582
James VI is imprisoned in Ruthven Castle (freed 1583). Shakespeare marries Anne Hathaway.

1583
Shakespeare's daughter Susanna born.

1585
Shakespeare's children Hamnet and Judith born.

1586
English courtier, poet and military commander Sir Philip Sidney killed at the Battle of Zutphen in the Netherlands.

1587
Mary, Queen of Scots, convicted of plotting against Elizabeth I, is executed. Drake destroys Spanish ships in Cádiz harbour and claims to have 'singed the king of Spain's beard'.

1588
Philip II of Spain attempts to invade England with his 'Invincible Armada'.

1589
James VI marries Anne (Anna) of Denmark.

1590
James attends the trials of the North Berwick witches.

1592
Earliest known reference to Shakespeare as a playwright.

1594
Prince Henry Frederick, eldest son of James VI, born. Shakespeare is now a leader of the theatre company, the Lord Chamberlain's Men.

1597
Shakespeare buys and restores New Place in Stratford. James VI publishes *Demonology*.

1599
James VI publishes *Basilicon Doron*, on the duties of kings. Globe theatre opens.

1600
James VI survives an assassination attempt, the Gowrie conspiracy. James's second son, the future King Charles I of England, born.

1603
Elizabeth I dies, aged 69. James VI of Scotland becomes James I of England. The Lord Chamberlain's Men become the King's Men.

1605
The Gunpowder Plot, a conspiracy to assassinate James I and his Parliament, is foiled on 5 November.

1606
Possible date of the first performance of *Macbeth*. Christian IV of Denmark, James I's brother-in-law, makes a state visit to England.

1610
Prince Henry Frederick becomes Prince of Wales.

1612
Henry, Prince of Wales dies, aged 18.

1613
The Globe burns down during a performance of Shakespeare's play *All Is True* (later called *Henry VIII*). It is quickly rebuilt.

1616
William Shakespeare dies in Stratford on 23 April.

Note: We do not know the exact dates of most of Shakespeare's plays, or even the exact order in which they were written. The dates shown here are only approximate.

1590: *Henry VI, Part I*
1591: *Henry VI, Part II*
       Henry VI, Part III
1593: *Richard III*
1594: *Edward III**
       Titus Andronicus
       The Comedy of Errors
       The Taming of the Shrew
       The Two Gentlemen of Verona
1595: *Love's Labour's Lost*
       Richard II
1596: *King John*
       Romeo and Juliet
       A Midsummer Night's Dream
1597: *The Merchant of Venice*
       The Merry Wives of Windsor
       Henry IV, Part I
1598: *Henry IV, Part II*
1599: *Much Ado About Nothing*
       As You Like It
       Julius Caesar
       Henry V
       Hamlet

1602: *Twelfth Night*
1603: *All's Well That Ends Well*
1604: *Othello*
       Measure for Measure
1605: *King Lear*
1606: *Macbeth*
1608: *Pericles*
       Coriolanus
       Timon of Athens
       Troilus and Cressida
       Antony and Cleopatra
1610: *Cymbeline*
1611: *The Winter's Tale*
       The Tempest
1613: *Henry VIII***
1614: *The Two Noble Kinsmen***

* May not be by Shakespeare
** By Shakespeare and John Fletcher

Shakespeare probably wrote two other plays, *Love's Labour's Won* and *Cardenio*, which have not survived.

'THE SCOTTISH PLAY'

Theatrical people are often superstitious, and many believe – or pretend to believe – that *Macbeth* is an unlucky play. Some will not even mention the name – they call it 'the Scottish play' instead. Here are some of the stories that are told about the supposed curse of *Macbeth*:

- It is unlucky to say the name 'Macbeth' inside a theatre.
- If you do, you have to go outside and spin round three times.

- It is unlucky to recite lines from the play outside a theatre.
- If you do, you can avoid the curse by quoting the same number of lines from Shakespeare's comedy *A Midsummer Night's Dream*, or the speech from *Hamlet* when Hamlet first sees the ghost: 'Angels and ministers of grace defend us!'
- The play is dangerous because the witches use real spells.
- Mysterious deaths have occurred during performances of the play.

MACBETH AT THE MOVIES

There have been many film versions of *Macbeth* – some straightforward performances of the play, others freely adapted from it. The earliest dates from 1916. Here are just a few of the better-known ones.

1948: *Macbeth* (USA)
A low-budget film directed by and starring Orson Welles.

1955: *Joe Macbeth* (USA)
The first of several adaptations set in present-day gangland.

1957: *Throne of Blood* (Japan)
Directed by Akira Kurosawa, starring Toshiro Mifune. A retelling of the Macbeth story set in feudal Japan. There are many departures from Shakespeare's plot, but it is considered to be a cinematic masterpiece.

1971: *Macbeth* (USA)
Directed by Roman Polanski, starring Jon Finch and Francesca Annis. Audiences were shocked by the film's violence and nudity, but many regard it as an intelligent and thought-provoking interpretation of the play.

1991: *Men of Respect* (USA)
A retelling of the story set in New York's gangland.

2003: *Maqbool* (India)
Set in present-day Mumbai, with the witches portrayed as corrupt policemen.

2006: *Macbeth* (Australia)
A violent film set in the Melbourne underworld, but using Shakespeare's original dialogue.

Jon Finch as Macbeth in the 1971 Polanski film

MACBETH TO MUSIC

There are two *Macbeth* operas: the famous one by Giuseppe Verdi (1847, revised 1865), and another by Ernest Bloch (1910). Dmitri Shostakovich's opera *Lady Macbeth of the Mtsensk District* (1934) is based on a Russian short story by Nikolai Leskov, not on Shakespeare. Richard Strauss composed an orchestral tone poem called *Macbeth* in 1890.

INDEX

FURTHER INFORMATION

IF YOU ENJOYED THIS BOOK, YOU MIGHT LIKE TO TRY THESE OTHER GRAFFEX TITLES:

Treasure Island by Robert Louis Stevenson, Book House 2006
Oliver Twist by Charles Dickens, Book House 2006
Moby-Dick by Herman Melville, Book House 2007
The Hunchback of Notre Dame by Victor Hugo, Book House 2007
Kidnapped by Robert Louis Stevenson, Book House 2007
Journey to the Centre of the Earth by Jules Verne, Book House 2007
Dracula by Bram Stoker, Book House 2007
The Man in the Iron Mask by Alexandre Dumas, Book House 2007
Frankenstein by Mary Shelley, Book House 2008

FOR MORE INFORMATION ON SHAKESPEARE AND MACBETH:

shakespeare.palomar.edu
en.wikipedia.org/wiki/Macbeth_of_Scotland